honestly,

lauren smoot

Dedication:

On the front cover of this book are forget-me-nots.
They say when you give these to someone
it holds the promise that you will always keep them in your thoughts,
and remember them.
So if this book happens to land in your hands,
know that you are not alone,
and be sure to let someone you love know that they are not alone either.

Contents

Painhub

Did It?

Did it have to shatter –
my world I mean.
For me to see that
it would not have hurt
as much, if I knew that
I could bloom as well.

Breakdown

It all starts with that inner need that wasn't met.

Soon it branches into fear, doubt, and mistrust.

Exhausted from all the racing thoughts

They go take what was supposed to be nap,

it turns into hours of lying still

The kitchen starts to feel too far away

but you wasn't that hungry anyway.

Feeling numb, you start pushing people away.

The phone is in your hands as you scroll away on it

but not enough energy to answer anyone.

By the time you realize it you are

met with your own tears of sadness.

Until something distracts you well enough

to help you disassociate,

and the cycle starts again.

Strangers, I Guess

I thought of you when I saw this…

I picked this up for you…

Did you eat today?

Let's go to our favorite place…

Wanna binge-watch…?

Remember when we used to…

Maybe next time then…

Message not delivered

Break to Break-Up

You suggested we take a break.

Those are risky, and we did it anyway.

You got to see other people, find yourself,

as people often say.

Drawing the same conclusions had

we actually talked it out.

I stopped hearing from you,

and decided to focus on myself.

Weeks turned into months, and it proved to be more

mentally exhausting waiting

for one another to figure out when our break

had been long enough.

Then your face showed up on my phone, and all I had to say was,

"So while we were on break I met someone and…"

Eldest Daughter's Curse

We all make mistakes,

but hers always receives the harshest punishments.

We all make mistakes,

but her apologies are not enough.

We all make mistakes,

but hers are made to be the hardest to learn from.

We all make mistakes,

but hers remind her that love is conditional.

Survival

The art of survival.

I am not stronger because I

survived all the trauma.

In fact, I am constantly

in pain from it.

I have the passive inner child

who now, screams to have the moments

back from before she was forced to grow up.

I have the obtrusive inner teen,

who will spit words of venom or fight

to defend that child.

Then you have the adult trying to pick up the pieces,

and instead, ends up disassociating

to find the balance between the two

I have a part of me that feels unsafe, another part that feels

rage for what happened, and the shell of a human

That has to figure out how to heal without

an apology.

Ghost Girl

Ghost girl is who she was.

People didn't see her for her.

People didn't hear her because

what she may say may be true.

People would avoid her because they saw others do it.

Because of this, she began to haunt.

She would make you finally see her.

She would make you finally hear her.

She would make you uncomfortable,

just as she was.

And then you will finally see that all this time,

she was asking for help with tears in her eyes.

The Sad Part

You know what the sad part is…

That I didn't need a choice to be presented to me,

to know that I would choose you.

You know what the sad part is…

that we've walked a similar path but,

mine is somehow viewed as less than yours.

You know what the sad part is…

that we both stayed instead of choosing to leave,

during different points in our lives

You know what the sad part is…

that you can't see my heart is bleeding

from showing how easy, it was to break.

You know what the sad part is…

that my voice is hoarse from yelling to be

seen and heard by you, yet still,

managing to be invisible.

You know what the sad part is…

we are unable to heal together.

I Bet You Think About Me

When you are treated poorly,

I bet you think about me.

I bet you think about my

kindness that you took for granted.

The way I always put your needs before mine.

I bet you think about how

I would've never said or did that to you.

I bet you think about how all of this

didn't have to be.

And I'd be wrong if I said I didn't

think about you.

The difference is I think of you

when I am treated how I was

always supposed to be.

My Heart

You held my heart in your hands.

It was wrapped around your neck

for safe-keeping.

Until, you cut the strings that connected us.

When my heart fell, it shattered into pieces,

and I learned that my heart needs to stay with me.

Time and Space to Heal

A band-aid with a kiss.

A suture with a story remiss.

A broken heart so complex to fix.

Takotsubo cardiomyopathy.

How can it heal within a set amount of time,

when the memories can last a lifetime?

Where can you find the space when

you are running out of it – all while

running from your thoughts?

Closure Isn't Real

I went back…

Thinking things could be as they were.

Thinking we could maybe get a redo.

A fresh, healthy start.

Only to have this nagging in my head,

pulling at my chest,

reminding me that the hole was

too big to fill with happiness,

but endless to be filled with pain.

Say My Name (In Your Sleep)

I hope my name never leaves your conscience.

I hope as my nightmares decrease,

your sleep paralysis demon drops mine

off as a gift.

I hope that you feel what I had to

endure ten-fold, and even then

I hope it finds you screaming for mercy.

Perfect Storm

Who would've thought…

being told that

crying makes you weak.

or being asked if you want

a reason to cry.

Or getting your heart broken

countless times,

could create such a

perfect storm in your chest.

More Tears

The older you get, the less you cry.

Then why can I remember crying a lot more

as an adult, than as a child?

You cry more as you get older.

As an adult there are so many more goodbyes,

falls, and moments that can bring happy tears.

There's that cry with no sound as an adult,

where you feel absolutely unheard.

There's that cry when you've finally found everything

you could ever want in a human being.

And it is then when you realize the tears were worth it.

Lovely Mess

What a lovely you've created darling,

all from overthinking.

If idle hands are the devil's playground,

then an overworking mind

must be the devil's amusement park.

Once the Dust Settles

Once the dust settles,

and I finally leave…

Will you finally notice

how much I loved you?

Will you finally notice

that you were every bit of enough for

me and I was not enough for you?

Or was it that I was too hard to love?

Will my absence leave a hole or will it just be like

I never existed like it is now?

Last Time

This is the last time.

The last time I cry this hard for someone,

who showed me just how much they care.

The last time I cry,

until I am hoarse and tired.

To the point where I'm begging

for the pain to stop.

This is the last time I let my

heart break for someone who

wouldn't even give me a piece of theirs.

Never Knew a Heart Could Break Itself

For what felt like years,

I've cried, and not just tears falling.

I screamed, I sobbed

until I was hoarse with despair

I could barely see by the time

I was finished, or so I thought.

Drowning in my sadness,

sleep a momentary escape.

But what made my heart break further

was knowing no one could relate to

me at this very moment.

Stop Making This Hurt

I wish I never told you what happened
because it did nothing but make me suffer more.
It did not change your actions but
it made all the difference when it came to me.
I reach for you for hugs to possibly
erase some of the disgust from his touch
but you reject every one.
So between the looks I get that makes me
feel broken, the hugs you wouldn't give to
remind me that I am safe,
and what I am left with now…
I find myself begging God or anybody for that matter
to make this pain stop.

Is God Watching the World Burn?

Is God Watching the World Burn?
Or is He waiting for us to take notice
that there is soon to be no more of it to burn?
From the selfishness, to the greed,
some things can be reversed, but instead
we look for another place
to make worse.

Sunset in my Pocket

Because you're not here anymore

I have to look at old pictures of you smiling,

to remind me of what heaven looks like.

That smile of yours was the

brightest of suns I could ever experience.

So I spend my days searching for

ways to chase the sun as I carry

a piece of you with me always.

The sunset in my pocket.

Show Me

Show me how to live again
without you here beside me.
Show me what it's like to love
to the fullest.
Show me how to believe in
myself the way you always did.
Show me how to be proud of
myself like you always were.
Show me, again, that
tough times don't last.
Show me I have what it takes
to live without you for now.

Kiss Me from Heaven

Every time I remember your smile,

it's like I received a kiss from heaven.

It comes with a memory, a small ache,

a flutter of happiness

that reminds me you are at peace.

As you pass my mind every day,

I can't help but think,

I can't wait

to see that smile again.

Love

Vintage

You bring the whiskey, I'll bring the wine.

You bring the warmth, I'll bring the passion.

You bring the heart of gold, and I'll bring

the love that never gets old.

You bring the amber flame, and I'll make sure

this attraction can never be tamed.

Drunk off of each other, utterly intoxicating;

I'm addicted to you.

Honey

Your words, like honey.

I stick to every single one.

Those sweet words

poured into my mouth,

with the lips to match.

It was easy to become addicted to you.

Your touch would have me

buzzing, aching for more.

And the honey would flow

from you, no effort at all.

Star-Crossed

I will never understand how we found each other.

Two very different worlds colliding,

somehow making beautiful poetry together.

The connection being too strong for

us both to handle, inevitably ending.

It was our fate, a painful one:

still one destined to be told among the stars.

Come Back Soon

Goodbye is too final,

it makes our journey feel over.

The adventure is just beginning,

and I have so much to share with you.

I will not say goodbye or see you later anymore.

Instead, I will say come back soon

so you will see how excited I

am for you to be with me.

Sweet Dreams

Let's have sweet dreams together.

We can forget about the world,

and indulge in each other.

You always know what to say

and the best part of you

and my dreams are:

I wasn't expecting you.

Glasses

The sun was in my eyes

but instead of using the sunglasses properly,

to be able to see you for what you are,

I used rose-colored glasses.

All because I knew it would hurt

my eyes and heart less.

Soft Landing

Pillows next to the couch,

pillows next to the bed,

all so you don't hit your head.

Helmets and knee pads are what you wear

to prevent any bumps or tears.

Practice makes perfect, and as we get older

we learn it was worth it.

But what do you protect your heart with

when you begin to fall hard?

Sweet Tooth

Your lips were sugar-coated with lies.

Your touch, an addiction, because

I was so deprived.

A craving that needed to be satisfied.

When I was close to seeing the real me,

I would be dipped into something more fascinating,

like a marshmallow in chocolate.

But it started to crack with pressure,

the cavities could not hide anymore.

To fix all the damage would take

more than braces or a fine piece of floss.

Sweetheart

Name something better than… (and I'll wait)

Feeling safe; reassurance;

Unconditional love; healthy boundaries;

Trust; privacy; your favorite food;

Your favorite song; your pet; your smile;

Your laugh, your person.

These all have one thing in common…

You

What could be better than you sweetheart?

About Love

Some things I know about love is…

Choosing your person should feel easy.

Being unshakably drawn to them.

Would never hesitate to find you in a crowd,

both figuratively and literally

Lying skin to skin feels just as euphoric.

Conversations go from shallow to deep, and

you both can go with its flow instantly.

Craving one another:

Never to the point of feeling suffocated.

Your love is freeing, the laughs are lifting,

And with one look,

you are feeling like you are home.

Hand-Me-Down Heart

It may be bruised, it may be battered.

It may have cuts, and it

may have a tougher exterior now,

but it is for protection.

It cannot take much more pain

Afraid that because it is broken,

you may not want it either.

I want you to have it,

as scared as I may be.

Why? Because you have shown

you can be gentle,

and that's what it needs.

All My Love

Slowly but surely,
all my love is coming back to me.
When I decided to choose myself,
I started to find pieces of me
along the way.
Each piece serving as a reminder
of what a treasure I truly am.

Sleepover

Can I sleep in your brain?

I want to ease the never-ending thoughts.

Can I massage all the tension away?

Can I peek at some of your fondest memories?

Can I look at some that you would like to forget>

I only ask this to know every piece of you.

The good and the bad.

I want to sleep in your brain to provide

your thoughts with comfort.

More importantly,

to erase any doubt that I love you.

Right Place, Wrong Time?

Right place, wrong time.
We could give it a try now but
would we make it?
We would find out what the purpose was though.
How long should we wait for the right time?
Life doesn't always wait for us to be ready.
So why not give it all we have now,
and maybe we won't leave
any questions unanswered.

Many Lifetimes

To meet you once
in twenty lifetimes is not enough.
My soul will always
search for yours in every lifetime
because our love spans
beyond dimensions.

The Right Thing

It is hard to let you go

but it's the right thing to do.

I have to do it for me

because it is no longer healthy.

I deserve better, but you do too.

Perhaps, this is just the wrong time for us.

I wish we could remain together, but if

we did it would destroy us,

and I love you more than I love myself.

If I Wasn't Yours, Who Was I?

It never occurred to me until now,

what I would do without you.

Until, I was shown what going

through these days would be like.

To see something funny, and see

that you're not there laughing with me.

To feel my heart breaking as I cry,

and see only I can pick up the pieces.

To hear my name be called, and hope

it was your voice.

I couldn't be me without you, so

if I wasn't yours, who was I?

The Wrong One

I wanted your love.

Your affection, your reassurance.

I wanted what money couldn't buy

from you.

That turned out to have a price too.

I asked for the bare minimum,

but even that seemed to be

too excessive of a request from you.

Can't Imagine a Better Feeling

For someone to squeeze your hand,

when you reach out to hold theirs.

For someone to return your hug,

and actually mean it.

For someone to match your energy,

at any given moment.

For someone to finish your thoughts and sentences.

For someone to notice you're not

acting or feeling like yourself.

For someone to understand, and

sit comfortably in silence with you.

For someone to say *I love you*

and mean it unconditionally:

Everyone deserves these things.

Far and Wide

Let's move to the top of a mountain,

where we can forget about all of our problems.

Let's go to the tropics,

just to fall asleep to the rain falling

Let's go to the highest floor with a balcony,

and lose our inhibitions.

Let's see the volcanoes

to remind us to release these feelings,

before we erupt

Let's move deep within each other's hearts,

so we'd never feel the need to move again.

Disastrous Love

Your love is a disaster.

Anger like a volcano ready to erupt.

Sadness like a tsunami I would drown in.

Intense like walking through a desert.

Heavy like the rain in the amazon.

Unpredictable like the jungle,

makes me shake out of anxiety.

Waiting for the earth to quake,

as I fight for your love.

I watch the cracks get wider

ready to consume me, and I realize this

is not loving me to the moon and back.

Rose Wrapped in Barbed Wire

My body wrapped in barbed wire,

so you cannot get close; you cannot hurt me.

Yet, I crave touch and affection.

My body wrapped in barbed wire,

so your words will only cut yourself.

My body wrapped in barbed wire

to protect me, unlike before, when I

was taken advantage of.

My body wrapped in barbed wire

became my new everyday wear.

The curve of the wire took the place of my smile.

It wrapped around my heart,

my throat so I could not be vulnerable again.

My barbed wire body.

As you peel away the wire, you are getting hurt too.

I can't bear to see it so I start to help remove it.

That was when I knew I had changed,

because I was ready to strip it all away.

Glimpse of Heaven

You paid me a visit in my dreams.

I was so happy to see you again.

It was the first time in a while I felt your warmth.

Little did I know, you came

with a message.

There, in your hand,

you were holding

a glimpse of heaven.

Leave

Take your love; it is not welcome here.

Take your love because it leaves me with despair.

Your love is not welcome here

because it comes with a price

If I love you I lose me, and I cannot do that twice.

Take your love, as it as it comes with conditions

that will never put me in a good position.

Your love is not welcome here

because it makes me feel tired and used.

Love is work but all you have to offer is an excuse.

Nights like Those We Had

Going out for ice cream
in the middle of the night,
will always be my favorite.
I always felt safest at night.
Like I could finally be myself,
and adding ice cream to it,
was the cherry on top.

Directions to Your Heart

Highway to your heart.

We don't know exactly where we're headed

we just know it's going to be memorable.

We have a bunch of stops to make,

but every exit reveals another exciting

path that leads to one another.

Something comforting about you,

where even sitting in silence is fulfilling.

So tell me which way are we headed today?

Your heart or mine?

Delusion

I don't know you like I used to
but it's probably for the best.
The way I knew you before
was unrealistic in a way.
I fell in love with your potential.
I used my own projections to create
a you that did not exist,
and that was not fair
to either one of us.

Snake Eyes

Eyes unreadable;

shell of who you used to be.

Craving your touch,

I let you wrap around me.

Staying focused on those eyes,

I didn't realize you were choking me.

No words could escape.

Then I saw you smile at me;

I woke up in a cold sweat.

And there you were sleeping

peacefully next to me.

How to Love

Ask if they ate today.

Tell them you miss them.

Find out their love language.

Tell them you love them.

Send what reminds you of them.

Help them clean if they need it.

Take a look from their perspective.

Be comfortable sitting with them in silence.

Do inner child activities with them.

Don't assume.

Never let go.

Fireworks in the Rain

Fireworks are a lot like us, you know?

Beautiful and mesmerizing.

Easy to get distracted by.

The echoing gets our heart racing,

and the bursts of color put on a good show.

However, an intense rain for us

can put them out or even stop us from lighting;

causing the show to stop.

Evergreen Love

My heart yearned for someone like you
to fill the emptiness of my heart.
I had to wait and be present
until my roots spread deep enough,
and until my trunk was strong.
Strong enough to stand on its own,
and feel refreshed after a rain.
Most importantly, be still enough to hear your heart
calling for me too.
My evergreen love.

Morning Mess

Alarm clocked snoozed for the third time.

Late and in a rush always.

Distracted by the morning anxiety.

Disassociating when you're supposed to be leaving.

Checking yourself in the mirror over and over.

Practicing the fake smile you plan to use,

to cover up everything else falling apart.

Forgetting to eat breakfast while also

remembering you would be nauseous if you did anyway.

But the moment you hear that voice you've

been dying to hear from,

anything feels possible.

The Hunt

They search for what they need
but keep finding what they want.
Impatience prevents them from
realizing they could have both.
Wisdom could whisper a hint
to these hearts of theirs.
That what they desire most will be
what they've needed and wanted
all along.

Will We Ever Get This Right?

Will we ever get this right?

Maybe when we're older.

Right person, wrong time.

Maybe when pride doesn't get in the way?

Who should apologize first?

Maybe when there's more love then obsession.

What can we do to fix this?

Won't You Stay Awhile

Stay and rest a while.

We don't have to talk about it.

Just your presence is enough.

Your mind deserves a break.

So let's go gather our favorite

snacks, hold onto one another,

and even if it's for a moment

forget how bad it hurts.

Choosing Yourself

Tangerine Dreams

Once that tangerine glow hit the sky,

she came alive.

She would peel off her guarded layer,

no longer caring who saw.

That smile couldn't get no brighter,

with a spirit as sweet as honey.

She couldn't wait to show you

what you've been missing.

A Perfectly Ruined Thing

What many people don't realize,

including myself, is the most perfectly ruined thing

is actually the moment when

you choose to second-guess yourself.

Remember before you hesitated,

it was perfect?

Summer Glow

Absorb all of that light.

Use it to heal and to take

with you into the night.

Give the night some of that light,

and you will see you were a star

as well, and just as bright.

Things You Outgrew Hearing

When you were always told to

honor your mother and father

but you learned that it also said

don't provoke your children to anger.

When it was do as I say not as I do,

but it became I can share some wisdom,

with the choice ultimately being yours.

When it was respect your elders,

but it became you get what you give.

When it was they're just overreacting or crazy

but it became this actually a reaction to

their trauma or feeling triggered.

When it will be you have the power to

make anything what you want it to be?

Borrowed Blue

Grey clouds and rose colored glasses,

surrounded by green.

Longing to be with the violets.

She was so blue you could

drown in her.

She learned her sorrow was borrowed,

and sought to find her real color.

Too Quiet

Is it too quiet?

Or are my thoughts too loud?

Is it too quiet?

Or am I just feeling unsafe?

Is it too quiet?

Or do I just need some reassurance?

Quiet is meant to be peaceful so

if it isn't, ask yourself what you need and I

guarantee it won't feel too quiet anymore.

Restless

A lot of change, a lot of heartache.

An uneasy feeling, hermit mode.

Changes in sleep, changes in diet.

New habits forming.

Something big is coming.

Making room for all

the manifestations.

Wait for Me

It's hard looking at what once was..

What used to be pure and innocent

Her smile, her laughter,

before it was taken away.

The hopes and dreams we shared,

now barely recognizable.

The fearlessness and the fierceness,

overshadowed by doubt and anxiety

Every time I reach out to her,

she's just slightly out of reach.

She almost hears me calling her

as she stops and takes a look around.

I almost call out to her again but

realize when I do I need to let her

take my hand and lead the way.

She will have to be the one to

remind me of everything I wanted,

and needed for myself.

Alone; Not Lonely

Lonely is what I was

when I was lying to myself.

Lonely was what I was

when I put up the façade.

Alone is what I am,

now that I've figured out who I am.

Alone is what I have to be

in order to heal.

Alone won't last forever but lonely will

because it means I am

finally putting myself first.

Lightning in a Bottle

For it to be safe for them,

they contained her.

She was unpredictable;

lightning in a bottle.

When you opened it, who knows

where she would strike next?

That's because her next strike could be

what would make her the perfect storm.

Before the World was Big

Before the world was big,

it felt like it was just you and me.

Holding hands and smiling,

not a care in the world.

For just a moment,

before the world was big,

all I could see was you.

And that was all that mattered.

I wish I could have a day like that again,

before I realized just how big the world is.

Lonely City

A lonely person in a lonely city,

full of love and potential.

Surrounded by untapped souls,

filled with greed and pettiness.

The person yearning to be heard and

understood for who they are.

Muffled by the sounds of

those happy in demonstrating

that their misery seeks company.

The lonely soul must escape this city

or, they fear they will face

a worse fate for not

wanting to conform.

Natural Disaster

They call her a disaster
because she's a tsunami
while often conveniently forgetting
how she was formed.
Like most tsunamis she was displaced;
she lost what she thought was home.
Her waves of heartbreak radiated outward.
Like most tsunamis her boundaries were
tampered with to add to her waves of despair.
All her choices were taken so
she took what control she had, and became
a natural disaster.
People forget that there is some good
that can come from tsunamis sometimes.
Tsunamis can redistribute nutrients –
she can put her life back together the way she wants.
Tsunamis can create new habitats –
she can create a new safe place for herself.
So natural disaster she may be,
she can use her strength for positive outcomes.

Graveyard Heart

I should have honored you,

my dear heart.

Now we're both frozen

in time and space.

Looking at the pieces

we call us.

I only get one of you.

I should have protected you more.

Instead all I did was shed

my skin to keep becoming

someone new.

But you,

you kept getting torn

and weaker understandably,

each time I used you to try

find the light.

Once in a Blue Moon

I will see a sign from you

whether that is a butterfly,

or a ladybug nearby.

A familiar feeling will pass

as if you're right beside me,

I get a warm and safe feeling.

As though, everything's going to be alright.

Every so often, once in a blue moon.

I am reminded I am loved, protected,

and guided by you.

Grey Skies

The sky was grey, but it felt like heaven.

The raindrops felt like happy tears,

knowing that a rainbow would follow.

Lightning would strike reminding

me to be spontaneous.

That, unpredictability, was not the end of the world

The thunder would remind me to make myself heard.

And once I understood the importance of

all of these, the sun would appear again.

Persona

Nothing shakes me, nothing makes me cry

I say as I do both.

Deep breaths, as I try to remind

myself I am in a safe place now.

I just got tired remembering

the fear, anxiety, and feelings from then.

But, I will apply my makeup, get dressed, and

convince the world that everything is perfect.

When You Ask Why

I take a good look at you
so I always remember what you look like,
especially while smiling.
I ask you for hugs often so
I can feel the need to stay.
I make you laugh often so you
will remember to do so even after I'm gone.

Living in a Sad Song

She was a pure child singing

a happy tune.

I had to watch her die.

She was a fearless teen

yelling her favorite lyrics.

I had to watch her die as well.

Now she is an anxious adult trying

to use the meaning behind the song

to heal her heart.

But all she can understand are the sad parts.

Follow the Leader

Follow me into the dark,

so you can meet the skeletons in my closet.

I am afraid you will leave once you know them all.

I have to take that risk because if I don't

I will become one of the skeletons myself,

and get locked in.

So take my hand I will lead the way,

and show you how all

my wounds came to be.

Seeing Red

Color me red

for the wounds both verbal and physical,

that still bleed.

Color me red

for the wrath I am feeling

that deserved so much more.

Color me red

for the passion that will give

me strength in showing others

that they are not alone.

Wilted

With you, I thought I found
my purpose in life.
Fragile like a flower
I would show you that even in your
worst moments there is beauty.
I would ignore the pain to
be the stem that could hold you up,
but you only watered yourself.
I would display my petals
to bring a smile to your face,
and you would pick them off
one by one with comparisons.
I would let the wind carry them
just to show you how far they could go,
and you would turn your head toward
a new flower for instant gratification.
What was left of me ached for light,
and instead was placed in a windowless room
until whenever you remembered me again.

Lonely in Love

It's lonely over here you know?

When you love this hard...

Not the immature shallow goals,

but the ones where we live out

everything we've ever wanted.

From childhood until now.

The kind of love that makes

loving yourself seem effortless

Yeah, it's lonely over here.

Dreamland Drowning

She slept to escape the racing,

the feeling of suffocation.

However, she didn't realize she was just sinking.

Those thoughts and feelings soon leaked

into her dreams.

A slow leak that would soon

prevent her from escaping:

Forcing her to finally make herself heard.

Mirror

I look at the three girls staring back at me.

The youngest with the most beautiful spirit and bright eyes.

She deserved to be treasured and protected.

I look at the imperfectly perfect teenager,

looking back at me cautiously and unsure.

She deserved to be reassured she was loved and safe.

I look at my reflection finally, and see that she is needed.

To show the past girls that those things weren't

too much to ask for.

Ocean

Every time I see the ocean,

time stands still.

I am drawn to the tide,

risking being pulled in.

Placing the seashell by my ear,

listening to the stories I am now

old enough to understand.

My soul is hypnotized, and instantly soothed

but aching to explore the depths.

True Blue

Blue is an excellent secret keeper.

The ocean keeps all the mysteries.

The sky holding all of the hopes.

Blue holds all the emotions,

that won't be said out loud.

Blue holds the tears,

threatening to spill.

The purest blue soul

often taken for granted.

Time to Fly

It's time to go, butterfly.

Spread your wings,

and leave the chrysalis behind.

You deserve to show the world

how much you've changed.

Though leaving behind the chrysalis

means saying goodbye to

some bittersweet memories, your

happiness awaits delicate creature.

Coming to Terms

I changed a lot of things since that day.

You don't know as much about me anymore.

You said I come first.

Now I am showing you what that actually looks like.

I never saw it coming.

The undoing of me, the broken pieces.

And although that day still makes me cry,

I am oddly at peace for finally

knowing and understanding the truth.

Good Things Fall Apart

Every time it falls apart,

I try to look for the pattern.

I make a better plan each time,

to avoid the destruction.

Almost like a maze or an obstacle course,

I try to break my own fall to

not make the landing as painful.

Then I learn that in order

for the good to start happening,

I have to feel the full fall.

When Did We Grow Up? Pt 1

When did we grow up?

When skip-its became skip class or work?

When outside all day turned into binge-watching?

When raising sea monkeys became raising kids?

When being called a picky-eater

was actually deeper than being *childish.*

When respecting your elders should have came with

the clause of treating people how you want to be treated?

When fitting in rightfully became

learning how to love yourself?

When Did We Grow Up? Pt 2

When did we grow up?

When we acknowledged people were mercilessly being fat-shamed

instead of being accepted as they are?

When nudity was viewed with shame,

instead of natural beauty?

When we realized the yelling and screaming

was unhealthy?

When we realized we acted like we did

but in reality, we didn't really trust each other?

When we realized the silent treatment

didn't help anyone see what went wrong?

When we realized this is not what

love should feel like?

When we grew up and as we grow,

I've learned is we need to use the things

we know now, for the child inside that deserves

a do-over.

I Was Wrong

I don't know you like I used to.

I used to think you would never do this to me,

make me feel this way.

Without so much as of an apology.

Then I realized it wasn't about who

I used to know

It was about me painting the image,

I wanted to see all this time.

Light

I keep this little light on

in the hopes that one day,

the room will be

so bright you ask for

a dimmer switch.

Worst Case Scenario

Tell me...

What do you say when

you're in the worst case scenario?

I survived.

Left Unread

Knowing how many moments

I needed you,

and you weren't there hurts.

However, it has taught me to show up

for myself first

because I wasn't there either.

Survivor of Nostalgia

When my heart starts to ache,

I realize I am a victim of nostalgia again

I am reminded of specific

people and places that

once brought a smile to my face.

I didn't want to move on.

Each renewed breath pulls me forward,

no matter how much I wish I could go back.

Me to Me

You deserve better.

It wasn't your fault.

You are worthy of the love you gave.

Others may not have deserved it.

You are safe now.

You will find your happiness one day.

There will be many rough days,

but you're almost there, and I know this

because I can feel it.

Somewhere deep down in my soul,

Our story still has yet to be told.

So stand up straight and get ready.

Reintroduce yourself to the world,

and this time, you will hold you steady.

Dear Diary: The Last Entry

I never knew all this time,

that all these tears I've shed

watered the roots to my tree of life.

And you know what?

I can't wait to see

what blooms.

Printed in Great Britain
by Amazon

84902983R00058